FAITH
WE PROCLAIM
IN THE
POSTMODERN
AGE

Dr. M. Nathaniel Anderson PhD

WESTBOW
PRESS®
A DIVISION OF THOMAS NELSON
& ZONDERVAN

This book is a work of non-fiction. Unless otherwise noted, the author and the publisher make no explicit guarantees as to the accuracy of the information contained in this book and in some cases, names of people and places have been altered to protect their privacy.

WestBow Press books may be ordered through booksellers or by contacting:

WestBow Press
A Division of Thomas Nelson & Zondervan
1663 Liberty Drive
Bloomington, IN 47403
www.westbowpress.com
844-714-3454

All Scripture quotations are taken from the King James Version.

ISBN: 978-1-6642-2471-1 (sc)
ISBN: 978-1-6642-2470-4 (e)

Print information available on the last page.

WestBow Press rev. date: 02/23/2021

CONTENTS

BIOGRAPHY

Dr. M Nathaniel Anderson, Ph.D. from Newburgh Theological Seminary an inspirational speaker, author, and entrepreneur, is known for his practical dynamic Bible teaching and powerful, prophetic preaching that cuts across denominational, cultural, and economic barriers. Dr. Anderson is Senior Pastor of the Power Christ full Gospel Ministries, a thriving, multiracial congregation in Severn, Maryland. He is also seen weekly on Step the faith, with Dr. Nate. On Face book live. As well as his weekly Everyday Faith Blog.

Dr. Anderson is a visionary and challenging leader who believes it is God's will for every believer to walk in prosperity and divine health through the power of faith. He is committed to helping educate people to what God's Word has to say about living and walking in victory.

Part of that commitment is demonstrated through the writing of this book faith We Proclaim in the Postmodern Age. It deals with the very heart of the gospel, the most important truth contained in the pages the Scripture. The just shall live by faith!

It is my hope and prayer that God will use this book to open the eyes of many to this central truth and lead them to experience, in this present life, the glorious liberty of the Son of God!

DEDICATION

I Want to Dedicate This Book to every person who truly desires to walk in faith--- body, soul and spirit. If you are one of those individuals, I believe you are holding in your hand a critical key to the doorway into your God ordained destiny of faith.

Whether you are a new believer or season believer this book, will be a powerful tool in the hands of anyone who is seeking to know the faith of Christ from a biblical foundation.

The gospel embodied is essentials to the gospel proclaimed if people are going to be reached and without doubt, an increasing number as churches are moving from the mire of the status quo to a new enthusiasm for extending God's kingdom.

Yes, I believe with my whole heart something new can happen again in the Body of Christ today! It is the evangelism movement, of faithful, loving and dedicated believers, who are being equipped and trained throughout the nations to share their faith. The Body of Christ is truly beginning to look like a mighty army. The Faith Revolution Continues, I believe this will continue to happen through effective evangelism in the postmodern age of the faith of Jesus Christ. This makes this book relevant and useful for today and future generations!

I cannot say enough about the work of faith, because that's what it will take, faith, faith is what He called us unto. The just shall live by faith and that alone will strengthen us and prepare us in the postmodern age of faith!

I know beyond a shadow of a doubt that you will experience the power faith operating in every area of the Body of Christ. As we continue to walk by faith in the postmodern age, of supernatural faith manifestation!

As you experience God's miracle power of faith in your life, please let us know here at M. Nathaniel Anderson Ministries how this life-changing book of faith has blessed you.

While you're at it, contact us at our ministry Facebook page. Power Christ for Gospel Ministries. And keep the faith!

INTRODUCTION

This theme brings light on the faith that is required in a postmodern age. New frontiers are carriers of faith undaunted faith that pertains to church growth, evangelism and missions. Frontiers represent uncharted territories that we are challenged to explore. This faith we proclaim will be imperative, for the development of church growth, evangelism and missions, in these new territories that are opening to present the faith of Jesus Christ.

So, as a church look ahead at 2020 and beyond, it will be the postmodern age, where the faith we proclaim must be without equivocation of the future kingdom. Three areas of focus will be represented in this assignment, along with the mission and message of the church. We will embark on postmodern church growth: How faith fit in the center of postmodern age. Postmodern evangelism: How Jesus method of evangelism is revenant to the postmodern advancement. And postmodern missions: How the upgrade of missions will affect the postmodern movement. In conclusion I will attempt, to bring clear understanding of the power of the faith we must proclaim in the postmodern age. And importance of faith that will be required to manifest global, church growth, evangelism and missions. In other words, the message of reconciliation is simply the gospel of Jesus Christ to the postmodern age, by the faith we must proclaim.

I hope to give clear assessment and thought to the idea that will be presented throughout the book, with the hopes of finding practical uses, in a world that still needs to be evangelized. It will also be my attempt, to show and present the importance of an ongoing need for Twenty first-century evangelism in our churches across the nation. As we proclaim faith in the postmodern age, a vital part of our spiritual existence. As I compile research from different sources in hopes of laying foundation of effective faith through evangelism that will summarize the importance of its urgency of the postmodern movement to a new generation of believers. It would be our solemn responsibility to not only participate in this evangelistic effort of faith, but to support it by the preaching of the gospel. My whole effort here throughout this book will be to show the efforts of evangelism, as well as the faith we proclaim in the Twenty first century and beyond.

THE FAITH WE PROCLAIM

The mission and message of the church: The power of the Christian faith is contained in the words of Apostle Paul: God was in Christ reconciling the world to himself, not counting their trespasses against them, and entrusting to us the message of reconciliation (Second Corinthians 5:19). Reconciliation is God's gracious act in Jesus Christ by which men are brought into right relationship to himself. That act has decisive importance for humanity; and the message of it is the gospel, the good news.

The Christian churches exist because God has acted to restore us, his conflict-ridden creatures, to fellowship with himself; and because he brings forth a new people in whom the hostility of men to men is overcome. This fellowship we called the church, makes up of the people who are entrusted with the ministry of reconciliation, because they had received God's reconciliation. The church carries out its mission in the knowledge that the same God who acted in Christ continues to act in the proclamation of the message. The church's mission is to direct men to God, the Father of our Lord Jesus Christ. It truly serves men and women by keeping before them God's redemptive act. Through the fellowship offered it to the lonely, it points to God, the Father who takes us into his family. Through its declaration of hope, it directs the despairing to God, whose conquest of evil to Jesus Christ gives hope to men. Through trustful reliance on God, it remains the anxious of God's providence.

1

Through its trust in the divine mercy and forgiveness, it leads the guilt ridden to God's mercy seat where forgiveness is found. By its ministry to the needs of men it testifies to God's love. By holding before men and society the demand for justice and peace, it testifies to the reality and sovereignty of God's order. The church cannot be itself unless it ministers to the world. And it cannot be true to its ministry unless it serves God in the service of men.

The church cannot be truly described as the community which testifies of God's deeds. It is the witnessing community, which is under obligation to give its testimony before men. Its testimony is to the whole range of God's mighty acts from his creation of all things visible and invisible to the climatic act of his renewal of man through Jesus Christ. It proclaims that God has made himself known to us, fulfilling in Jesus Christ his saving purpose declared through his prophets; that in the self-sacrificial love of Jesus Christ, God has declared his holy love; that he gives to us his Spirit and eternal life.

The church testifies too many acts of God; but its witness is that God's act in Jesus Christ is decisive significance. The conviction of Christian is that God has come to us in holy love and creative power in Jesus Christ. The church proclaims what it has found and continues to find truth: In Christ, God himself comes to us, meet us, brings us into fellowship with himself and gives us a share in the goodness and power of his divine life. Christ is the fulfillment of God's saving purpose. He fulfills the knowledge of God, for the knowledge of God he gives is the knowledge of communion; and because that is so, the knowledge of God we have received through Jesus Christ is the standard by which all knowledge of God is tested. Because Christians have received fellowship with God through Christ, they are convinced that God invites us to fellowship with himself through Christ's invitation.

The witness of God's acts does not end with the divine deed in the earth the ministry, crucifixion, and resurrection of Jesus Christ. It continues with the testimony concerning what God now does within man. God's sending of Jesus has its sequel in his gift of the

Spirit, who works within man to awaken faith, to renew his life, to liberate him for a life of responsibility freedom, to guide him into truth, to strengthen him in goodness, and to unite him to fellowship with faithful people.

Thus, the Christian testimony takes the form of a recital of God's acts, all of them bearing upon his saving purpose, disclosing his mercy and judgment, his power and his goodness. The crown of all his acts is his coming to us in Jesus Christ who brings us with him into God's own presence, through whom we receive Sonship, the Spirit, and eternal life. And to what he has done and is doing, the recital adds what he will do: he will complete the new creation he has already begun. That expectation is the Christians hope which sustains faithful people in bearing the conflicts and tragedies of life in history"[1]

The mission of the church-evangelism (Acts 2:47). Praising God and having favor with all the people. And the Lord added to the church daily such as should be saved. The first and foremost work of the church is evangelism. Evangelism is the work of calling and leading people into the saving knowledge of Jesus Christ. This work is so important it was reported in the book of Acts as one of the first milestones of the faith. And the Lord added to the church daily, such as should be saved.

Pentecost has fully come, and the disciples were now living in the power of God's divine assistance. The power of God had done a new thing. People who were afraid to witness to others about Jesus were now bold and powerful in their faith. The purge of new life had come upon the disciples just as Jesus promised it would do. Believers were now constantly being added to the church and ready affirmation of God's outpouring of Pentecostal power.

A recent report in our news media has told how the Protestant mainline churches in America had all suffered major decline in their membership. The mainline churches such as the Presbyterians, Episcopalians, American Baptist, Methodists, have all seen that overall level of membership declined rapidly. However, there is a growth in church life many may not know about. According to a recent survey documenting Christian growth in America and reported in the Washington Post, the Pentecostal Church of African American in America has grown faster than any other group. We hear about some of these God and certain word churches, but we do not hear much about the rapid growth of the Pentecostal churches of Christ. These churches are growing because the people find in them a living and burning fellowship. They are growing because people come to their church expecting to see and to witness signs and wonders. They believe that the church makes a difference in their lives. They believe that God is more than a theoretical discussion for a theological classroom. They believe that God is real. They believe that his Son Jesus Christ did die upon the cross. He was raised of body from the dead. He is calling for his people to live holy. He is coming back again. That is always the design and practically of every generation, for the church to be postmodern. Some want to ignore the Word of God and do those things that are popular and please the desire of the people. This is why our text is so important. It tells us about the work of the church in its first generation of witnesses. It tells us what the Christian believers did as they began the process of reaching the world with the gospel of Jesus Christ. Faith we proclaim in the postmodern age: responses to God's acts. God, to whose mighty acts the church testifies, is active; he is, in biblical phrase, the living God. His acts are themselves the evidence that he is working still (John 5:17). Thus God is neither passive nor is he so remote from us that he does not take an active part in the course of man's life.

He, who creates, renews, judges, and saves, takes the initiative in disclosing himself to us. God is not one who waits passively for man the seeker to discover him. Rather he actively seeks out man in order to disclose himself. He takes the initiative in engaging us in dialogue, and often himself for our communion, and is giving us knowledge of himself. This will be key in the postmodern age, our knowledge of God, as the Christian community teachers, is based upon God's own activity of revealing himself. He is the God who discloses himself; our knowing him is our response to his act of making himself known. Whatever important may be assigned to the role of religious genius or insight and to reflective thoughtful wisdom, the critical matter is the primary of God's act in making himself known in the postmodern age.

Faith, understood as trust in God, is our personal response to God's disclosure of himself. The faith of Christian church, understood as the beliefs held about God, has its source in God's self-revelation. Faith is confidence, not in the knowledge we have gained, but in God who has, to us. The faith we hold is not the statement of our own discoveries; rather it is the account of him who finds us even when we hide from him. The postmodern age will still center on knowing him.

God reveals himself, in this postmodern age and he who makes himself known to us is he whom we are seeking. He finds us and, when we know we are found, we know that our search is ended in a fulfillment immeasurably greater that our highest expectations.

The faith we proclaim in the postmodern age is the Christian gospel proclaim as the good news of God's reconciliation act bring us into communion with him. It is not the report of human insight or wisdom. Indeed, if by religion is meet man's search for God, then the Christian gospel is not a religion but rather the end of all religion. For the heart of the gospel is that God come to man to redeem and to renew him, in the postmodern age, but compels us to know him even greater in the postmodern age.

But such a sharp antithesis between man's search for God and God's search for man in the modern age, as if the two were mutually exclusive, contains our as well as truth. The search for God is itself in some measure a response to God's seeking for man. God, who prompts man to seek him, is he who revealed the fullness of his grace in Jesus Christ. This will not stop in the postmodern age, but will spread, as we proclaim faith in the postmodern age.

God takes the initiative in giving us knowledge of him. He is not passive, merely waiting to be found, but active in his self- disclosure. Thus, our knowledge of God differs in kinds from our knowledge of nature gained using scientific methods. In seeking knowledge of nature, we the investigators, are active and nature is passive. We might speak of discovering truth about nature; we do not speak of nature's revealing itself to us.

Although knowledge of God is different in kind from the knowledge we gain by scientific method, however, the church in the postmodern age will have no quarrel with science. On the contrary, the church is concerned to promote and to undergird science. Moreover, it is not true, as some honestly believe that commitment to the Christian faith is a hindrance to scientific investigation. Rather, to hold that Christ is the principal of unity of all things provided as far more adequate basis for objectivity than does non -commitment.

The church in the postmodern age, does not take issue, however with those who denied the possibility of revelation and the validity of any knowledge of God whatsoever. Science makes no such denial, in this age though some have wrongly thought that signs either required or supported denial of the possibility and validity of any knowledge of God. Clearly justice now attacks the very foundation of Christianity. For divine revelation is the basic of the Christian faith. The faith in the postmodern age will not change this divine revelation but strengthen the faith of the Christian church.

Revelation at its highest and best was given in Jesus Christ. Faith in the postmodern age will strengthen and bring greater clarity. It was given in an historical person, born in the region of Caesar Augustus and crucified under Pontius Pilate. Christians, consequently, are intensively interested in the historical Jesus: his time, his teachings, his actions and, preeminently, his person. The faith we proclaim, is our vital concern and does not, of course end with knowledge about Jesus. Our goal, in the words of Paul, is that I may know him and the power of his resurrection, and may share his suffering, become like him in his death, that if possible I may attain the resurrection from the dead (Philippians 3:10-11).

This will not change in the postmodern age. Because Jesus Christ is center of the Christian faith, we need to consider the source of our knowledge of him, and the postmodern age. That source is the Bible

The faith we proclaim in the postmodern age, will still center on the fact that Jesus is Lord. Paul sees himself as one of these men. Before his conversion experience he had been intent on pleasing God, committed to this great objective and doing his dedication best to fulfill it, yet the darkness in which he lived was so deep that when he saw and heard Jesus, he didn't recognize him as the Son of God but thought him to be a usurper and a vagabond. But on the road to Damascus he was suddenly overwhelmed with light. Out of the darkness of his brilliant mind the light shone and illuminated the darkness of his dedicated heart. There he experienced what he has long sought, the knowledge of the glory of God. And this experience will still be available to all who come to God in the postmodern age. To his utter amazement he found it where he least expected: in the face of Jesus Christ. God set aside young Saul's brilliance, his dedication, and his blameless morality as having done nothing to advance him on his search for reality. Suddenly it was all made clear Jesus is Lord! There will be no difference in the postmodern age of faith. Using that key, everything began to fall into place; the universe and life itself began to make sense. And the best of all, Paul's found his self-fulfilled as a man. Jesus was real and was with them night and day. Prayer and power were his as a daily inheritance, enriching his life beyond all expectation. He had found the secret of God likeness.

Because of his own experience the apostle is careful now to keep his preaching sharply the focused on the only subject God will honor by calling light out of darkness, that is, we preach not ourselves, but Jesus Christ as Lord, with ourselves as your servants for Jesus sake. The danger in preaching is that all too often we offer ourselves as the remedy for man's need. We speak about the church or Christian education or the Christian way of life, when all the time what people need is Jesus. This will not change in the postmodern age of faith. The church cannot save, knowledge of Christian philosophy does not heal, and doctrine without the puffs up, only Jesus is Lord, only he is essential to life. When he is encouraged all the other things will fall into their proper places. Faith in the postmodern age will bring even greater light to a dying world, in the postmodern age.

FOLLOWER OF THE WAY

Living a Christian life in the postmodern world, if you look at the New Testament, you find that the early church lives in a culture that is much like the one we live in today. There were no absolutes and when the Christians claimed that Christ was the only way that was pushed back by the secular society. Here are some suggestions for collective as we see to be a witness in this present culture.

The living a godly life postmodern, early Christians understood that they could make a difference by living a godly life before and unbelieving world. We also need to be above reproach in the way we live our lives before unbelievers. Believe me; they are watching to see if that is any difference between you and them. When we choose to compromise our faith by the decisions we make, by what comes out of our mouth, and how we treat others, it hurts our witness. The radically sold out to Jesus Christ.

Knowing the truth by studying God's Word, if you truly want to have an answer to those who knew little of the Christian faith or the difference it can make in their lives, study the Bible. Get a good Bible translation that you can understand and began to read it. Memorize meaningful Scripture passages, proclaiming the truth of God and love. We do not need to sit back and not proclaim who Jesus is and what he has done in our lives. If you have been transformed by Jesus Christ, you are a new creature. You need to proclaim that true. But do it in love. Be kind, not judgmental.

Not long ago, I met a young man who was struggling with very serious moral issue. He came in and we talked for quite some time. He let me coach him or how to escape from the sin that was destroying his life. At the end of the session, he thanked me for being kind to him. When we deal with people and proclaim Christ to them, we need to be loving. Remember God hate's the sin but love the sinner. This will be paramount, and the postmodern age of faith.

Quit riding the fence when it comes to your faith. There's nothing worse than a hypocrite. Don't pretend in your Christian faith. Be sold out. Remember that Jesus himself said that he was the only way. This is not changed in the postmodern age of faith. He is not one way; he is the only way. That way is narrow. His call for commitment and dedication, but we don't go it alone. God is right there with us, guiding us along the way. Faith in the postmodern age will continue to provide the way.

If you truly want to change the world, do it through Jesus, who calls us to transform the world. He calls or us to spend our lives in the service of the least, the lost, the lonely. Following Jesus is about putting into practice the things that Jesus taught. If we do that, the world will take notice. And that world in the postmodern age will be of the faith of Jesus Christ.

A life of faith in the postmodern world, millions of people throughout the world call themselves Christians. From Roman Catholics to Protestants, from fundamentalist to liberals, they are many different perspectives about what is meant to be a Christian. One can become lost in the complexity of the beliefs, dogmas, moral injunctions, and religious rites. But in a larger context that of daily life it is often impossible to distinguish one's Christian from another, or even a Christian from a non-Christian. Most Christians blend in with the values, lifestyles, economics and politics of the predominant culture in their society. But it was not always this way. Once upon a time, Christians stood out from the crowd.

The way of Jesus, like many other great religious leaders, Jesus taught a way or path to his followers. His teaching pointed to an understanding of the religion life as a journey. He spoke about alternative paths encountered on the journey the wide path and the narrow path. He talked about seeking and entering the kingdom or reign of God. These are active words. They imply doing something, moving from where we are to someplace new. They are not words to correct beliefs and doctrine, but words that call us to get up and get going. Jesus called people to follow him in a way of living. This will not change the faith in the postmodern age. As a result, the early as members of the Jesus movement were known as followers of the way. And this way will not change for those of the postmodern age of faith.

Believing all following, will still be a relative importance in the postmodern age. Lots of people believe in Jesus. They just love him to pieces. They worship and adore him. They praise his name. Invite him into their hearts and accept him as their Lord and Savior. But not many people are willing to follow him. For the most part, believing in Jesus is believing things about Jesus that Jesus is divine, that he died for our sins, that he will come again to judge humanity and to establish his kingdom.

But this kind of believed is not necessary take the teachings of Jesus seriously. One can conceivably believe that Jesus is the Son of God and yet still live self-centered lives, ignoring the cries of the poor, the demonstration hatred towards people of other races, cultures, or sexual orientations. All this believing, loving, worshiping, and accepting Jesus is largely an internal experience, sometimes highly emotional, and although it's frequently expressed in a corporate setting, it's often intensely personal and private. But following Jesus is not an internal state. It's an engagement with the outside world in a tangible way.

Some Christians are embarrassed to discuss their beliefs, while others are more than willing to profess their faith in public. This will be important in the postmodern age of faith. Some may wear a cross as jewelry to symbolize their faith and devotion to Jesus. But public proclaim a Jesus Lord is still not the same as following Jesus.

Why do you call me Lord, Lord, and do not what I tell you? Jesus once asked Luke 6:46.

Following Jesus is about listening and doing. It's about putting into practice the things that Jesus taught. It is about a lifestyle of peace and justice that set one apart from others.

Churches often put a focus on discipleship. However, it's been said that some churches that claim to be teaching discipleship adjust making good church people. The call to increase worship, study, and stewardship often result in people who simply serve the institution of the church.

Being a disciple should be radically different from being a disciple. It involves much more than worship attendance, Bible study, or service on the church board. Admittedly, those can be important parts of the Christian life. But they are merely food for the journey, not the journey itself. Hopefully they provide nourishment, not a detour.

Discipleship should result in people who lead a radical different type of life, who are counter-cultural, who are markedly different from the rest of the world. Jesus called us to transform the world. He called us to spend our lives in the service of the least, the loss and lonely. That kind of life goes way beyond serving in a local congregation. The content of true discipleship is found outside of the walls of the church. It is found what people are hurting, what people are hungry, what people are oppressed, what people are denied justice, what people are dying. This realization will not go away in the postmodern age. However, true faith in the work of the cross will better prepare us for the task ahead.

Now, the issue before us is whether we want to move from being admirers, or even worshipers, being followers in a postmodern world. If we want to take a step, then the question is what does it really mean to be a follower of Jesus today? Is Christianity a set of beliefs, or is it a way of life? If it is a way of life, what kind of life? Is it delineated by clearly drawn moral rules, or is it a compassionate respond to the situation that confronts us?

What does a life of faith that is honest to Jesus, look like? Even more precisely, how will this life of faith be expressed as we entered the postmodern world? We live in a very different age than the pre -modern people Jesus spoke in the first century. The modern age, which began in the Enlightenment of the 18th century, is now rapidly becoming a postmodern age.

Despite a seeming chasm between the first century and the twenty-first, the way of Jesus is as appropriate to the postmodern world as it was to the pre-modern world. But it will not be achieved by clinging to a pre-modern worldview as some conservative Christians do today.

The earlier paradigm is still the majority force in America Christianity today, but it is no longer speaking to millions of Christians who are uncomfortable with his definition of the faithful life. This earlier paradigm causes many to wonder if they can still call themselves Christians if they don't buy into biblical literalism, religious exclusively, and a heavenly afterlife as a goal of the Christian life. However, the millennium will again gravitate to a life of faith in the postmodern world.

Following Jesus in the postmodern world involved a radical different understanding of the identity, mission and message of Jesus than the traditional understanding presented by the earlier paradigm of Christianity. Following Jesus in a postmodern world it bought a new set of answers to the following three questions: who was Jesus? What did he hope to accomplish? What did he proclaim? If we are able to rediscover the life and teachings of Jesus in a fresh way, to understand how Jesus confronted a social issues, politics, economics, and religion of his day, we may be able to bridge the gulf between the ancient world and the postmodern world.

THE DOCTRINE OF FAITH

To perceive and value the treasures of the church, one must enter through the experience of faith, the teaching of faith in the postmodern world. It would be very easy to draw of notebooks of complaints, full of things that are not going very well in our church. But this would be to adopt an external and depressing vision, not to see with the eyes of faith, which are the eyes of love. Of course, we should not close our eyes to things that are not going well, but we need to understand the overall picture in which the problems to be resolved are situated.

This is a unique period in church history. As we consider the present situation of the church with the eyes of faith, we see specially two things. First, there has never been in the history of the church a period as fortunate as ours. Our church has is graded geographical and cultural spread and yet finds itself substantially united in the faith, except for Lefebvre's traditionalists. Second, in the history of theology that has never been so rich a period as the last era. Even in the fourth century, the era of the great Cappadocian fathers of the Eastern church and the great fathers of the Western church, like St. Jerome, St Ambrose and St. Augustine, there has not so great a theological flowering.

It is enough to recall the names of Henri de Lubac and Jean Danielou, of Yves Congar, Hugo and Karl Rahner, of Hans Urs von Balthasar and his master Erich Przywara, of Oscar Cullmann, Martin

Dibelius, Rudolf Bultmann, Karl Barth and of great American theologians like Reinhold Niebuhr, not to mention the liberation theologians (whatever judgment may be made and their regard now that they are being given new attention by the Congregation of the Doctrine of the Faith) and many other still alive, including the great theologians of the Eastern church of whom we know too little, like Pavel Florenskij and Sergei Bulgakov.

They can be very different of nuanced views of these theologians, but they certainly are an impressive group such as never existed in the church in times past.

All this has taken place in a world full of troubles and challenges, such as the unjust distribution of goods and resources, poverty and hunger, and the problems of violence and maintaining peace. Other problem is the difficulty in fully understanding the limits of civil law in relationship to moral law. These problems are very real, especially in certain countries, and they are often subject to a very lively dialectic of interpretation.

Indeed, sometimes it is possible to imagine that we are not all living in the same historical age. Some are still living in the time of the Council of Trent, others of the First Vatican Council. Certain people have digested the Second Vatican Council well or poorly; others are well advanced into the third millennium. We are not all true contemporaries, and this has always been a great burden for the church and requires plenty of patient and discernment. Yet we would like to put these problems aside from now and consider how pedagogical and cultural situation and the problems associated with education and teaching postmodern world.

There is a postmodern mentality. To seek a fruitful dialogue between the people of this world and the Gospel and to renew our pedagogy in the light of the example of Jesus, it is important to look closely at the so-called postmodern world, which forms a backdrop for many of these problems and which conditions the solution.

A postmodern mentality could be defined in terms of oppositions: an atmosphere and a movement of board that stands opposed to the world as we know it until now. This mentality willingly distances itself from metaphysics, Aristotelianism, the Augustinianism tradition and from Rome, considered as the center of the church, and from many other things.

This mindset keeps its distance from the former Platonic Christian world, in which there has taken for granted the primacy of truth and values over feelings, of intelligence over the wheel, of the spirit over the flesh, of unity over pluralism, of asceticism over life, of the eternal over the temporal. In our world there is a spontaneous preference for feelings over the will, for impressions over intelligence, for an arbitrary logic and the search for pleasure over an ascetic and prohibitive morality. This is a world in which sensitivity, emotion and the present moment come first. Human existence, therefore, is a place where there is freedom without restraints, where a person exercises, or believes he or she can exercise their personal empire and creativity.

At the same time this movement is also a revolt against an excessively rational mentality. From literature, painting, music and the new human science (psychoanalysis), many people no longer believe they live in a world ruled by rational laws, in which Western civilization is a model for the world to imitate. It is accepted that all civilizations are equal, whereas previously we insist on the so-called classic tradition. Nowadays there is a little of everything on the same plain, because there are no longer criteria by which to verify what is true and authentic civilization.

There is opposition to rationality, which is seen as a source of violence, because people believe rationality can be imposed because it is true. There is acceptance of every form and dialogue and exchange because of a desire to be always open to others and to what is different, to be suspicious of oneself and to mistrust whatever wishes to affirm its identity through force. That is why Christianity is not easily accepted when it is presented itself as true religion. I recall the young man who said to me recently: above all, don't tell me that Christianity is true. That upsets me that block me.

It's quite something to say that Christianity is beautiful. Beautiful is preferable to truth.

In this atmosphere, technology is no longer a means of humanity's service, but a milieu in which someone perceives the rules to interpret the world. There is no longer an essence of things, but only the use of things for certain and determine by the will and desire of each person.

In this atmosphere, the refusal of sin and redemption is always present. It is said, everyone is equal, and each person is unique. There is an absolute right to be singular and to affirm oneself. Every mole rule is out update. There is no more sin, nor pardon, nor redemption, nor self-denial. Life can no longer be thought of as sacrifice or suffering.

A last characteristic of this movement is the refusal to accept anything that smacks of centralism or a desire to direct things from on high. There is an anti-Roman complex in this way of thinking. We had passed from a context in which the universal counts for more; what was written and general and timeless, what was durable and unchanging was referred to what is, local and dated. Today, the preference is for a knowledge that is more contextual, local, pluralist, and adaptable to different circumstances and different times.

We do wish to say all this is completely false. A great deal of discernment would be needed to distinguish the truth from the false, what is said as an approximation for what is said with precision, and that which is simply a tendency or a fashion from what is a solid declaration. What we are saying is that this mentality is everywhere, especially when they are young people, and it needs to be taken into account.

There is something more, perhaps this situation is better than one that existed previously. Christianity has an opportunity to show better of challenge, of objectivity, of realism, of the exercise of true freedom, of a religion linked to the life of the body and not only of the mind. In a world such as we live in today, the mystery of an unavailable and always surprising God acquires greater beauty;

faith understood as wrist becomes more attractive; a tragic view of existence is strengthened with happy consequences in contrast to a purely evolutionary vision. Christianity appears more beautiful, closer to people, and yet more true. The mystery of the Trinity appears as the source of meaning for life and an aid to understanding the mystery of human existence.

To teach the faith in this world is nonetheless a challenge. To be prepared one must take to heart the following attitudes:

Do not be surprised by diversity. Do not be frightened by what is different or new but look upon it as something which is found a gift from God. Prove that you can listen to things quite differently from what we usually think, but without immediately judging the speaker; try to understand what is being said and the basic arguments put forward. Young people are very sensitive about an attitude of nonjudgmental listening. This attitude gives them the chance to say what they really feel and began to distinguish what is really true from what only appears true. As St. Paul says, examine everything with discernment; key what is good; keep your distance from every trace of evil (First Thessalonians 5:21-22).

Take risks. Faith is the great risk of life. Whoever wishes to save his life will lose it; but the one who loses his life for my sake will save it (Matthew 16:25). Everything must be given up for Christ and his Gospel. This will not change in the postmodern age of faith. Befriend the poor. Put the poor at the center of your life because they are the friends of Jesus who made himself one of them? Nourish yourself with the Gospel. As Jesus tells us in the discourse on the bread of life: for the bread of God is that which comes down from heaven and gives life to the world (John 6:33). And the faith in the postmodern world will continue in this wise.

Talking about faith postmodern, faith is waning in the West, and these words are but a few examples of how some people view faith. According to the British Social Attitudes survey, over half of the British populations proclaim no faith. As Muslim who are heavily involved in their faith and interfaith communities, one wonders how to convincingly talk about the force of faith which still means so much too so many people. Meanings are sought after. In a world characterized by increasing polarity, preconceived lack of control, and the looming threat of climate disasters, faith is a precious commodity that can provide some order in our tumultuous, ever-changing world. Irrespective of whether one follows a faith or not, it is difficult to deny the weighty, existential meaning that faith provides. The narrative and beliefs of faith are upheld through the ritual, which creates and ethical framework within which resilience can be assessed in a turbulent world.

As we look at postmodernism: The Spirit of the age. We live in strange times. Christianity was under fire because it was thought to be unscientific and consequently, untrue. Today, Christianity is widely rejected, not because it was critically examined and found wanting, but merely because it claimed to be true. Increasingly, American academics regard claims to be objective and universal truth as intolerant and uninformed. What accounts for this bizarre and growing consensus? It's called postmodernism. Postmodern ideology rejects the authority of reason and views all claims as objective truth to be dangerous. For these enormously influential thinkers, truth is political and created by belief communities, not discover rationally or objectively. That the academic community is experiencing a major ideological revolution is beyond doubt.

Like all intellectual movements, postmodernism deeply effects the broader culture. In this paper will show how popular religion views mirrors academic postmodernism, then clarifies the challenge of this new consensus for the church, as it heads into the postmodern age of faith.

Abigail Van Buren has provided America with practical advice on almost every problem imaginable. Nowhere does she advises reflect the spirit of the age more than religion. A few years ago, dear Abby provided advice about how to handle religious disagreements. In it, Abby entertained the following criticism of the previous published column. Abby's response captures a growing consensus about religious tolerance and faith commitments. Two principles implicit and her comments show how thoroughly the postmodern hegemony in academics is fueling cultural attitudes. First, entry into religious controversy is, in her words arrogant. Second, personal choice is the ultimate basis for spiritual truth. Understanding these new, broadly held convictions, is essential both for reasoning non-Christians in our culture and for the ongoing vitality of Christian church. Rule number one, it's arrogant to suggest that someone's religion beliefs might be wrong. By arrogant, most people mean intolerant a term that has come to have a whole new meaning in recent years. Intolerance used to refer to bigotry or prejudice. That is, judging someone or excluding them because of who they are. In this sense, intolerance is offensive. But now, intolerance means that simply disagreeing about beliefs is wrong. The recent movie" At play in the Fields of the Lord "illustrates this point. In a conversation between an Amazonian Indian and a Christian missionary, the Indian says, if the Lord made Indians the way they are, who are you people to make them different? This is one of the defining sentiments of our day. Attempting to convert is unacceptable because it implies standing in judgment over other 'beliefs.

The only exception clause to today's code of tolerance is criticizing what is pejoratively labeled fundamentalism. Fundamentalism does not mean what it did in the early decades of the century. Nor does it refer to religious extremism, like the Shiites' holy war against the West. Today, fundamentalists are those who believe that religion truth are objective and therefore subject to rational investigation.

We are witnessing a broad-based backlash against reason in our culture. This backlash is widely promoted in contemporary higher education. The argument is that every time somebody claims to be in process of the truth (especially religious truth), it ends up repressing people. So, it is best to make no claims to truth at all.

Rejecting objective truth is the cornerstone of postmodernism. Postmodern ideology declares an end to all ideology and all claims to truth. How has this seemingly anti-intellectual outlook gained such wide acceptance in history's most advanced civilization? That question requires us to understand how postmodernism conceive the past three hundred years in western history.

Postmodernism abandons modernism, the humanist philosophy of the European Enlightenment. In light men thinking is based on the authority of French philosopher René Descartes 'autonomous man the one who starts from his own thoughts (I think, therefore I am) and builds his worldview systematically from reason alone. Naively, postmodernists charge, modernists assumed that the mind was a mirror of nature, meaning that our perception of reality actually corresponds to the way the world is. From this presumption, modernists built a culture that exalts technological achievement and mastery over the natural order. Expansion minded capitalism and liberal democracy, outgrowths and modernist autonomous individualism, subjugated the earth to the Eurocentric, male dominant paradigm.

But modernism planted the seed of its own undoing. As arrogant, autonomous modernists conquered the global and subjugated nature in the name of progress, oppressed and marginalized people have responded. Progress toward what? They cry. Postmodernists says that the idols autonomous reason technological proliferation have brought the modern age to the blink of disaster. The myth of progress ends up in a nightmare of violence, both for marginalizing people and for the earth.

Enter postmodernism, postmodernism rejects modernism's autonomous individualism and all that follows from it. Rather than seeing humanity as an ocean of individuals, postmodernists think of humans as social constructs. We do not exist or think independently of the community with which we identify. So, we can't have independent or autonomous access to reality. All of our thinking is contextual. Rather than conceiving the mind as a mirror of nature, postmodernists argue that we view reality through the lens of culture. Consequently, postmodernists reject the possibility of objective truth. Reality itself turns out to be a social construct or paradigm. In the place of objective truth and what postmodernists call metanarratives (comprehensive world views), we find local narratives, or stories about reality that work for particular communities but have no validity beyond that community. Indeed, postmodernists reject the whole language of true and reality in favor of literal terms like narratives and story. It's all about interpretation, not about what's real or true.

Postmodernists hold that the pretense of objective truth always does violence by excluding other voices (regarding other worldviews to be invalid) and marginalizing the vulnerable of scripting them out of the story. Truth claims, we are told, are essentially tools to legitimate power. That's why in postmodern culture, the people to be feared is the ones who believe that we can discover ultimate truth. The dogmatist, the totalizer, the absolutist is both naïve and dangerous.

A growing number, especially among the emerging generation, believes that reason and truth are inherently political and subversive. That's why they are often so cynical. According to the voices in contemporary culture that shape Generational X thinking, claims to truth are clever disguises for the pernicious will to power. Consequently, rather than dominate others without version of reality, we should accept all beliefs as equally valid. Openness without the restraints will reason, and tolerances without moral appraisal are the new postmodern mandates.

European history is a mixed. Postmodern critics of Enlightenment humanism accurately draw out the legacy of autonomous (and fallen) human beings. But at the same time, it's hard not to be struck by the shallowness of the postmodern line of argument. If tolerance means that we can't offer criticism of other beliefs, and then invectives direct it towards those who believe in objective spirit and truth seem out of bounds too. Common assertions that Christians are arrogant for accepting the universality of biblical truth turn out to be profoundly intolerant.

Rule number two, you can't separate the beliefs from the believer. Anymore, that rejecting the content of faith means rejecting the person holding it. Because truth now means personal preference and personal empowerment. It's no more appropriate to question the validity of a person's belief than to critique their source from the dinner menu. Simply believing is justification enough. Striving together to discover spiritual of truth through debate and spirited discussion is out, because no real different exist between what a person chooses to believe and what is true for them.

Consider current opinion about the religions of the world. Few people understand much about them. Yet conventional wisdom is what they all teach pretty much the same thing. The real concern is finding spirituality that fits. George Barna's research shows that.

America is a religious smorgasbord. The only question seems to be what are you hungry for? And Chase is more important than substance. That's why people are largely unmoved when it is pointed out that their beliefs are often the hopelessness contradictory or that they live inconsistently with them.

For most people, the postmodern outlook they described as more absorbed than thought out. An impressive majority of Americans believe the truth is relative. But few know why they think that way. Still fewer have any clue about how they beliefs practically relate to their own lives. In general, people are more ideologically confused and deeply committed to their convictions. So, while we hear the rhetoric of openness to everything and tolerance for everyone, it's rare to find someone who really understands what this means. It's just the socially appropriate attitude you have. Postmodern ideologues have been successful in transforming ideology into popular zeitgeist.

Ironically, in an age of anti-dogmatism, this radical subjectivity leads to the dangerously arrogant inference that no one can ever be wrong about what they believe. We are free from the constraints of rationality; nothing separates truth from self-delusion. The age of anti-dogmatism ends up being the age of anti-intellectualism. The tyranny of truth has been replaced, even amongst academics, for self-empowering stories. And these stories typically function at the expense of truth.

Christians need to be respected for what others believe and of the traditions and experience that form those beliefs. But the postmodern demand to uncritically accept all religious beliefs as true (at least for the person who believes them) is fanatical. Beliefs form in the postmodern claims of openness and tolerance creates a firewall against genuine and substantive dialogue about spirituality and moral truth. History offers sobering testimony to the high price such anti-rational dogmatism.

Significantly, postmodern subjectivism also inhabits a deep commitment to one's own beliefs. Since faith is rooted in the practical matters of personal taste and experience, the tendency is to adopt and abandon believes according to the demands of the moment. Remember, truth is a human creation, not something we discovered independently of ourselves. So, if the truth no longest satisfies, just move on to something new. How tragic it is when we are told by friends and neighbors that, I tried Christianity for a while, but it just did not work for me.

SPIRITUALITY AND THE CHURCH

Postmodern spirituality and the church., this new conventional wisdom has enormous implications for the future of evangelical Christianity in America we see two disturbing indications that the church is increasingly becoming conform to the culture's postmodern mold, as an educator and pastoral leaders.

First, while the culture is more open to spirituality now than in the past several decades, the church is substantially unprepared for effective evangelism. Evangelicals have been slow to discern the spirit of the age. Consequently, many in our community approach spirituality from a postmodern perspective. It's disturbing to note, regarding Barna's survey on religious syncretism cited earlier. So, what about the task of evangelism? If all religions are simply culturally conditioned avenues to the same God, then no one is really lost. Spirituality is not really darkness, but merely a different shade of light. Barna notes that the logical contention of this syncretism is a growing lack of interest in evangelism.

We don't know of any evangelical scholars or pastors who teach universalism. And the hallmark of the evangelical church is a passionate commitment to evangelism. So how have so many evangelicals come to think this way? Much like everyone else it's is absorbed through uncritical participation in postmodern culture.

Nowhere has this absorption of postmodern ideology has been evident than with the emerging generation. Thoughtful Christians recognize that this generation lacks meaning for exposure to the gospel more than any previous generation in American history. But without the unwavering resolve of the church, fueled by deep conviction that the gospel is absolutely true young men and women will not be reached for Jesus Christ. The last thing this generation needs is the way postmodern consensus to guide the church.

When dealing with college student arguably some of the most cynical people we will meet. We found that their relativism and postmodern critique of culture are less conviction and more like the party line they have been indoctrinated with. Working with them is peeling back the last of an onion. We hear the reasons why true is dangerous and how reason is merely an oppressive western construct. But in conversations, sooner or later you get to the core of deep help beliefs that they accept as objectively true. For all but a deep committed few, postmodern theology is a veneer. Understanding postmodern reason and having thoughtful responses to its enables Christians to effectively communicate the gospel of Jesus Christ.

The second concern about evangelicals today is while the church is distinct from the culture in terms of how we think about those values. It's good that the church instilled biblical morals. But what grip do we have on them? When a substantial percent of our congregations rejects spiritual absolutes, what sustains our attachment to moral absolutes? For many Christians, values are merely a part of their identity with Christian subculture.

There is a necessary connection between spirituality truth and moral absolutes. Because God is infinite, personal Sovereign of creation, his nature is the only objective foundation for ethical values. To the extent that truth about God is cast in terms of culturally relative beliefs, biblical mortality must follow. And there is indication that the erosion of objective values is suffering the same decline in the church of objective spiritual truth.

As this observation indicates, we are paying a very high price for being engulfed to buy postmodern culture. But the solution to the challenge of postmodernity is not to run from secular society. That's really not an option says it is neither possible nor biblical. Abandoning true is not an alternative either. At a time when the culture is enamored with the idea of personal empowerment, of evangelicals need to gain an appreciation for the power of ideas and the skills needed to take them captive to the obedience of Christ.

The church has been appropriately sensitive to the personal danger incurred by people living in a socially and morally fragmented age. Christian therapy and pastoral counseling are a mainstay in most of evangelical churches today. But for the sake of the ongoing effectiveness of the church with this culture, we also need to attend to the ways people approach matters of truth. Having a solid grasp on the postmodern ideology and the coherent, biblically response to it are now imperative for reaching the lost and raising men and women to spirituality. This will be undertaking, for faith in the postmodern age. Remember the wisdom of Apostle John in a very similar age. I have no greater joy than this, to hear of my children walking in the truth Third John 4.

Now the postmodern world, the world in which we live is changing. For the past three hundred years we have been part of the age call modernity. The modern age is now giving way to the postmodern age. This transformation will change how people view the world, how they understand reality and truth, and how they approached the fundamental question of life. This will have a tremendous impact on Christianity. The church has its roots in an ancient pre-modern Mediterranean worldview. Slowly it's has accommodated is self to the modern world. But many critics wonder whether it will be able to survive the shift of the postmodern age.

Postmodernity is a different reaction to modernity. Postmodern its people are essentially disenchanted modernist. They're convinced that reasons and cleverness cannot achieve the happiness we seek. They had witnessed the environment to ravages of the industrial revolution, the blood he history of the twentieth century, and continued misery, poverty and hunger around the globe. None of these problems were solved by scientific knowledge. On the contrary, the byproduct of science and the industrial revolution exacerbated many of the problems. science is providing cures to disease, but it has not created the threat of global warming and nuclear annihilation, in fact, the bombing of Hiroshima and the resulting nuclear arms race they had been the spark that marked the demise of modernity and ignited the rapid rise of the global postmodern culture.

But, unlike fundamentalism, postmodernism does not seek to return to an earlier time. Nor does it see a return to authoritarian religion as the answer. Postmodernism is characterized by the belief that both religion and science have failed us. Neither can be trusted to provide the answer to life's mysteries or to solve life's perplexing problems. Nonetheless, the faith we claim will be paramount as we move into uncharted territories in the twenty first century and beyond. In the postmodern worldview, people become their own authority accept only what they personally experience. There is a sense that feeling is all that counts because, in the end, feeling is all that is. Postmodern attitude is, if I can feel it, if I can touch it, then it must be true. This is not the faith that we proclaim in the twenty first century. Our faith will be solely based on the truth of God's word.

Historical epochs are not neatly separated. They are not line up end to end. It is possible to continue to live in an era that is essentially over. While one era prevails, its successor is already forming, and its predecessor source continues to exert influence for a very long time. However, we must remember that the influence of faith we proclaim is from faith to faith which is eternal.

These three worldviews pre-modern, modern, and postmodern coexist side-by-side today in all parts of American culture. But it is particular apparent in our churches. Some Christian accept what they are told by religious authorities. Others question authority and use reason as a guide. Still others reject institutional religion and trust only their own spiritual experiences. But regardless of generations, culture, or attitudes, we all are moving together towards postmodern world. And the movement is rapidly accelerating. And the faith we proclaim will be a very big part of the generation, culture and attitude of the modern church or the generation Y that will carry the faith moving even further.

The most fundamental of Christian understanding is found in the Creed develop by the Christian church in the fourth century. (Faith). This Creed develop over many years at two ecumenical councils (325 AD and 381 AD) is called the Nicene Creed. It is shared by almost all Christians across time and space. It served as basic understanding of the Christian movement. (Romans 1:17). The just shall live by faith. We believe in one God, the Father, the Almighty, maker of heaven and earth, of all that is seen and unseen. We are invited to explore the meaning of the most basic and fully ecumenical understanding of the faith as found in the Creed.

Karl Barth sums up his conception of the theologian 's attitude towards philosophy nicely in these words: All things are lawful to me, but nothing saves the word of God shall keep me captive.

In Barth second publication of this critical decade in Barth's development was demands attention and perhaps Barth's least read book. In 1930, Barth left Munster to become Professor of systematic theology at the University of Bonn. There he continued his practice of offering seminars on the history of theology. One of the first seminars dealt with Anselm's Cur Deus Homo. This precipitated further study of Anselm and his theological method. In 1931, these labors bore fruit in Barth's book on Anselm's proof for the existence of God within the context of his theological program entitled Fides quaerens intellectum (faith in Search of understanding).

Faith we proclaim will be in search of understanding in the postmodern age of real faith in the word of God. I believe this is why Barth held Anselm in such high regard. In the preface Barth states that he considers Anselm's proof for the existence of God to be a perceptive and sound piece of theology, which, if heeded, could be instructed both for the modern Protestant and Catholic theology in terms of what constitutes an adequate theological method. It is noteworthy that at the outset of the important section in the church dogmatic dealings with the knowledge of God Barth wrote I learned the fundamental attitude to the problem of the knowledge and existence of God at the feet of Anselm. Put more generally we can say that Anselm helped Barth developed the theological method characteristics of the entire church dogmatic. In short, Anselm taught how theology could be done. If we are to understand faith, in the postmodern age which will be relevant to the life of the believer now and forever. We must be concerned as Barth's was in his analysis of Anselm's theological method is evident in the title of his study, Fides quaerens intellectum, which is the original title of Anselm's Proslogion. This Anselmic phase is a variation of Augustine's dictum that unless you believe, you will not understand. The critical problem for theological method here is: what is the relationship between faith and knowledge, or why does faith seek understanding? Or we could put it a bit differently and ask: How do we move from the moment of faith to theology? Barth holds that a polemic and apologetic intention does motivate Anselm's desires for understand. But neither this nor the joy which accompanies the clarification of one's faith through reason provides the primary motivation for this quest.

Barth follows Anselm in holding that faith seeks understanding because this movement is characteristic of the nature of faith as such. Barth summarizes this drive of faith for deepened understanding and more certain knowledge of God, its object, as follows: Credo ut intelligan (I believe in order that I might understand) means: it is my very faith itself that summons me to knowledge. And this will not change as we go forward in faith proclaiming our faith in the postmodern age.

Barth reminds us that in order to comprehend how the program of faith seeks understanding is carried out, we must understand Anselm's concept of faith. Faith is not to be confused with something irrational or illogical. Barth paraphrases Anselm's understanding of faith as follows: faith is the right act of the will if it is that which is owned to God and demanded by God, and bound together with a saving experience: that is, in so far as it is faith in God, in so far as its beliefs that which is true. Faith comes from hearing and hearing comes from preaching. Faith is related to the Word of Christ and it is not faith if it is not the reception, that is, knowledge and acknowledgment of the Word of Christ.

For Barth and Anselm, therefore, we do not begin our quest for knowledge of God apart from faith. Rather, we must begin with faith in the Word of Christ or the Word of God which has been spoken. The Scriptures and ancient church Confession are the highest expressions of the churches Credo or faith. The individual Christians faith (credo) must hold to the understanding of Christ in these norms if it is to be true faith.

Barth sees the progression from faith to understanding in Anselm something like this. First, at the initial level of faith there is a certain knowledge or understanding concerning the words which proclaim Christ. This is an intellectual comprehension which even the unbelievers may share. But in the second place, faith moves beyond this logical understanding of the true at firm to an understanding of the reality behind the words. Thus, in faith, Christ who is proclaimed is acknowledged. Faith, then, stands both at the beginning and the end of the quest for understanding: we move from faith to faith. Expressed otherwise, is the quest for understanding on the part of the believer moves from faith toward sight, an apprehension which will be fully realized only in the eschaton.

Barth contends that it is precisely because the beginning and the end of the process of understanding are present in faith that theology is possible. The success or failure of faith attempt to reach most complete understanding in no way threatens its existence. That is good news for proclaim in faith in the postmodern age. For theology exist neither to lead one to faith nor to free from doubt. Nor does it tried to storm the heavens or requires a sacrifice of one's intellect. The theologian can do his task and the recognition that all humans' knowledge of God, including that contained within the Confession (Credo) of the church, is dependent for its validation upon the revelation of God

FAITH JESUS WAY

This revelation, of living our faith, in the postmodern age of faith is found in (Matthew 28:18-20). Then Jesus approached and said to them, all power in heaven and on earth has been given to me. Go, therefore, and make disciples of all nations, baptizing them in the name of the Father, and of the Son, and of the Holy Spirit, teaching them to observe all that I have commanded you. And behold, I am with you always, until the end of the age.

The mission of the church drives is organization, not the reverse. This mission is entrusted not only to the faith community but to our ecumenical sisters and brothers as well. Together we endeavor to proclaim the Good News of Christ in our words and actions to one another and to the person who are not associated with the faith or religion.

Young people of the third millennium must be a source of energy and leadership in our churches and our nation. Therefore, we must provide young people with an academically rigorous and doctrinally sound program of education and faith formation designed to strengthen that union with Christ and his church. Christian schools can collaborate with parents and guardians and raising and forming their children as families struggle with the changing and challenging culture and moral contexts in which they find themselves. By equipping our young people with a sound education, rooted in the Gospel message, the Person of Jesus Christ, and rich in the cherished traditions and liturgical practices of our faith, we ensure that they had the foundation to live morally and uprightly in our complex modern world. This unique identity makes our elementary and secondary schools for the human person and allows them to fill a critical role in the future life of our churches, our country and our world in which we proclaim the faith of Jesus Christ."[13]

When we speak up authentic Christianity, we are speaking of a life of faith in the postmodern age. Only authentic faith will move God's promises into the earth realm. Therefore, millions of people throughout the world call themselves Christians from Roman Catholics to Protestants, from fundamental this to liberals, there are many different perspectives about what is meant to be a Christian. One can become lost in the complexity of beliefs, dogmas, moral injunctions and religious rites.

But in a larger context, that of daily life, it is often impossible to distinguish once Christian from another Christian or even a Christian from a non-Christian. Most Christians blend in with the values, lifestyles economic and politics of the predominant culture of their society. But it was not always this way. Once upon a time, Christians stood out from the crowd.

Faith the way of Jesus: Like many other great religious leaders, Jesus taught a way have to followers. His teaching pointed to an understanding of the religious life as a journey. Spoke about the alternative paths encountered on the journey the wide path and the narrow path. He talked about seeking and entering the kingdom or reign of God. These are active words. They imply doing something, moving from where we are to someplace new. These are not words of correct beliefs and doctrine, but words that call us to get up and get going. Jesus called people to follow him in a way of living. As a result, the earliest members of the Jesus movement were known as followers of the way. And that was the way of faith that still holds significant value now and will continue to hold value in the postmodern age of faith.

Lots of people believe in Jesus. They just love him to pieces. They worship and adore him. They praise his name. They invite him into the hearts and accept him as their Lord and Savior. But not many people are willing to follow him, in the way of faith. For the most part, believing in Jesus is really believing things about Jesus, that Jesus is divine, that he died for our sins, that he will come again and just humanity and to establish his kingdom. But this kind of belief does not necessarily take the teachings of Jesus seriously. One can conceivably believe that Jesus is the Son of God and yet still live self-centered lives, ignoring the cries of the poor, and demonstrate hatred towards people of other races, cultures, and sexual orientations.

All this believing, loving, worshiping, and accepting Jesus largely an internal experience, sometimes highly emotional, and although it's frequently expressed in a corporate setting, it's often intensely personally and private. But following Jesus is not an internal state. It's an engagement with the outside world in a tangible way.

Some Christians are embarrassed to discuss their beliefs, while others are more than willing to profess their faith in public. Some may wear a cross as jewelry to symbolize their faith and devotion to Jesus. The publicly proclaiming Jesus as Lord is still not the same as following Jesus. Why do you call me Lord, Lord, and do not do what I tell you? Jesus once asked. (Luke 6:46). Following Jesus is about listening and doing. It is about putting into practice the things that Jesus taught. It is about a lifestyle of peace and justice that sets one apart from others.

Churches often put a focus on discipleship. However, it's been said that some churches may claim to be teaching discipleship are just making good church people. The call to increase worship, study, and stored ship often result in people who simply serve the institution of the church. However, the faith that we proclaim in the postmodern age will extend far beyond these areas that appear to the outside world but will translated beyond the walls.

Being a disciple should be radically different from not being a disciple. It involves much more than worship attendance, Bible study, or service on the church board. Admittedly, those can be important parts of a Christian life. But they are merely food for the journey, not the journey itself. Hopefully they provide nourishment, not a detour' discipleship should result in people who lead a radical different type of life, who are counterculture, who are markedly different from the rest of the world.

Jesus calls us to transform the world. (By faith). He calls us to spend our lives in the service of the least, the lost and the lonely. That kind of life goes way beyond serving in the local congregation. The content of true discipleship is found outside of the walls of the church. It is found where people are hurting, where people are hungry, where people are oppressed where people are denied justice, with people who are dying.

In a book called the Cost of Discipleship, Lutheran theologian Dietrich Bonheoffer (1906 -1945) described the difference between cheap grace and costly grace. Cheap grace, he says, is grace without a commitment and responds from the believer. It is grace without servant hood. Costly grace, Bonheoffer, moves us to respond to the call of Jesus, by faith. Danish philosopher Soren Kierkegaard (1813-1855) called the typical Christian response of mine Christ instead of following Christ. The issue before us is whether we want to move from being admirers, or even worshipers to being followers or a faith follower of Jesus Christ. If we want to take that step there the question is what does it really mean to be a faith follower of Jesus today?

Is Christianity a set of beliefs, or is it a way of life? If it is a way of life, what kind of life? It must be a way of faith. It is delineated by clearly drawn moral rules, or is it a compassionate response to the situation that confronts us? What does a life of faith, that is honest to Jesus, looks like? Even more precisely, how will this life of faith be expressed as we enter the postmodern world.

We live in a very different age than the pre-modern people to whom Jesus spoke in the first century. The modern age, which began in the Enlightenment of the eighteenth century, is now rapidly becoming a postmodern age of faith. Despite the seeming chasm between the first century and the twenty first, the way of Jesus is as appropriate to the postmodern world as it was to the pre -modern world. But it will not be achieved by clinging to pre-modern worldview as some conservative Christians do today.

In his book the Heart of Christianity, biblical scholar Marcus Borg (1942-2015) described two very different ways of seeing what the Christian life is all about, two different visions of Christianity. Borg describes these as an early paradigm and an emerging paradigm. The earlier paradigm is still the majority for in America is Christianity today, but it is no longer speaking to millions of Christian who are uncomfortable with-it definition of the faithful life. The earlier paradigm causes many to wonder if they can still call themselves Christians if they don't buy into biblical literalism, religious exclusivity, and a heavenly afterlife as the goal of the Christian life. The emerging paradigm has been developing steadily for the last century and has become a kind of grassroots movement within the mainline denominations. Borg is careful to say that the issue is not that one of these paradigms is right and the other is wrong. Rather, the issue is functionality, whether a paradigm works or gets in the way.

Nevertheless, following Jesus involved a radical different understanding of the identity, mission and message of Jesus than the traditional understanding represented by the earlier paradigm of Christianity. Following Jesus in the postmodern world involved a new set of answers to the following three questions who was Jesus? What do you hope to accomplish? What did he proclaim? If we are able to rediscover the life and teachings of Jesus in a fresh way, to understand how Jesus confronted the social issues, politics, economics, and the religion of his day, we may be able to bridge the gulf between the ancient world and the postmodern world.

Postmodern church growth and how faith fits into the center of the postmodern age. This will be done by the pouring of new wine into new wineskins a culturally relevant ministry. Most people read essays for different reasons. Some people laugh because it's nostalgic. It reminds them of the good old days when life seems so much simple and easier. These Pre boomers make up the generation that preceded the Baby Boomers Generation. They are the Harry Truman Generation. Of the people that because they take much of what is said for granted. They tend to assume that life has always been like it is today. This group consist of the Baby Boomers and the Baby Buster Generations. They are the Pepsi generation (with apologies to the Coca-Cola Company).

What all of this depicts is change. Times have changed dramatically! And there's more much more to come. In terms of information alone, George Barna notes that we now have only 3 percent of the information that will be available to us by 2010. Someone has said that, currently, the amount of knowledge doubles every five years! Obviously, all this massive change has deep the influence our culture. Like going to 1940s and 1950s is completely foreign to the life at it is in the 1990s and as it will be in the twenty century.

As our world changes, the evangelical church must change as it attempts to communicate the message of Jesus Christ. The culturally leap from the unchurched community to most American churches is too vast. Consequently, our planted churches must be culturally relevant if they're to reach this and future unchurched generations for the Savior. They must be relevant when they begin, and they must remain relevant.

The mature church must be willing to be flexible in areas that relate to its unique culture (the world in here), but not in areas that relate to biblical truth. There are two in areas which a church can adjust in response to changes in the world out there. It changed what it believes (faith), and it can change what does (practice). The first area has to do with fundamental principles of belief and doctrine. The evangelical church for the most part holds to Scriptures as its authority and the basis for what it believes. Since biblical truth is eternal truth, the church and not must not compromise the principle of Scripture. So, what will postmodern age mean for evangelism. The principle applied today, yet, strangely enough; it is scarcely comprehended in practice today. Most of the evangelistic efforts of the church begin with the multitudes under the assumption that the church is qualified to preserve what good is done. The result is our spectacular emphasis on numbers of converts, candidates for baptism, and more members for the church, with little or no genuine concern manifested towards establishment of these souls in the love and power of God, yet alone the preservation and continuation of the work.

Surely if the pattern of Jesus at this point means anything at all, it teaches that the first duty of the church leadership is to see to it that a foundation is made in the beginning on which can be built and effective and continued evangelistic ministry to the multitudes. This will require more concentration of time and talents all feel people in the church while not neglecting the passion for the world. It will mean raising up train disciples of the work of ministry pastor and church staff (Ephesians 4:12). A few people so dedicated in time will shake the world for God. Victory is never won by the multitudes.

Some might object to this principle when practiced by the Christian workers on the ground that favoritism is shown towards a select group in the church. But be that as it may, it is still the way that Jesus concentrated his life, and it is necessary if any lasting leadership is to be trained. Where it is practiced out of a genuine love for the whole church, and do concern is manifest towards the needs of the people, objections can at least be reconciled to the admission be accomplished. However, the goal must be clear to the worker, there can be no hint of selfish partiality displayed in relationship to all. Everything that is done with the few is for the salvation of the multitudes.

EVANGELIZING POSTMODERN AGE

Evangelism postmodern, the mention of the word postmodernism evokes them notion of pluralism, where anything goes, since the concept to becomes relative. This then poses a real challenge is to the Christian one-way method of salvation, where the Bible clearly provides evidence of Jesus asserting, I am the way, that you and your life. No one comes (to God) to the father, except through me (John 14:6). Later, Apostle Peter echoes these were about apology: there is salvation in no one else, for there is no other name under heaven given among men by which we must be saved (Acts 4:12). These absolutes of the Christian message suffered in the advent of modernism worldview and now suffered more from postmodernism. The question that begs an answer is: what does postmodernism mean for evangelism today? We must begin our discussion with a historical survey that will trace the winding path through which postmodernism has come to us. This will then lead to the question of evangelism in the postmodern world. Evangelism, Jim Leffel captured the spirit of the age of postmodernism aptly: Today, Christianity is widely rejected, not because it is critically examined and found it wanting, but merely because it claims to be true. Increasingly, Americans academics claims to objective the universal truth as intolerant and uninformed.

This poses a challenge to evangelism, since in it one seeks to convert another. How can one attempt to convert someone to Christianity seeing that each person is entitled to his or her own beliefs? To evangelize them would be viewed as religious intolerance, or as Leffel puts it: Attempting to convert is unacceptable because it implies standing in judgment over another's beliefs. A survey carried out in America shows that the majority of people think that all religions pray to the same god and therefore no one is really lost. This thinking has entered the church through the back door and hence there is no commitment to evangelize the amount many evangelicals.

The challenge of postmodernism culture to must be dealt with at the congregational level by igniting the spirit of evangelism amongst believers. (Romans 10:14-17) is a wake-up call to believers to evangelize. The messages of the gospel must be heard in order to bring the desired effects of conversion. The seed, the word of God, needs to be scattered by someone (Luke 8:5). The harvest need not be aware of his readiness; it is the farmer who knows when to harvest. In the same way, the church must pray for the owner of the harvest to raise up harvesters even in these days of postmodernism, which is supposedly rejected, and religious freedom advocated.

We must adjust all methods of evangelism if we are to reach the young people today. The older people are still sympathetic to the gospel, but the young ones in a culture that is bent towards accommodation. All faiths are taken to be personal and hence are being seen superior to the others.

Although the postmodern worldview rejects absolute truth and advocate for wide choices of religion, there remains an open door in the heart of many. People are looking for solutions to meet their problems and the gospel that comes to meet that need will find room in many hearts today. Like Jesus, it is important evangelists to propagate the gospel through the open door of felt needs. Jesus always reached the hearts of the people by meeting their felt needs, whether they were physical, social, emotional or spiritual. If the evangelist knows God, knowing self and knows the people, he or she will be an effective communicator of the gospel. Postmodernism calls for a subtler mode of evangelism. No church can turn back the clock to premodern times. The declaration of thus said the Lord must be clothed in an attractive coat. Bearing in mind that although the core of the gospel does not change, the method must suit the context. If there was ever a time to contextualize theology, this is the time. The church must understand the time that postmodernist is living in and seeking God's help to meet the challenge of communicating the gospel to them.

Postmodern missions, how the upgrade of missions will affect the postmodern movement. Many churches demonstrate that God honors the commitment to missions. Local evangelistic efforts need not conflict or compete with missions giving for causes around the world. This shows that local evangelism and worldwide missions can be both/and instead of either/or. Mission minded churches truly do baptize more!

Community, a postmodern mission paradigm? So, to answer the question this statement, the words community, postmodern, mission and paradigm are examined in turn of defined. The central place of the local church in contemporary missiology is discussed, and the need for a missional and communitarian ecclesiology is argued with positive but crucial reference to the approach of the gospel and our culture network of North America. This thought in this by suggesting that communities can indeed be seeing as a mission paradigm for postmodernity, and posing questions facing the local church it is to be, a missional community.

Missionary teaching in the postmodern context will be crucial. Actions really do speak louder than words, especially for first-term missionaries' tongue -tied with learning a new language and adapting to a culture. The discipline of learning from others even in our roles as teachers is especially relevant in a postmodern age that emphasizes community-based decisions making over unequivocal authoritarian control. As David Dockery notes, for the new postmodern generations to consider the plausibility of Christianity, they must be convinced of is authenticity, as well as the community building characteristics, before they will hear is to claims (1997, 17). We can model and practice such authenticity if we intentionally take learning posture in our teaching.

Unfortunately, taking a learning posture with others is often viewed as a weakness instead of a strength. But if we want to teach others to understand and his or biblical truths into that thoughts and lives, we must present them incarnationally. Postmodernism crying out for authenticity in life, not simply a well-ordered presentation of theological propositions. Authentic living requires that we admit our shortcomings and place ourselves in situation where we ask questions and learn from those, we are teaching. Thus, we model ability and the value of community-based instruction, of the strength in the postmodern context. This approach has been especially helpful in a cross-cultural setting. Students and persons alike feel valued and understand they have something to contribute, while they are also challenged to see a perspective that may better fit with their own evangelical faith.

This raises two suggestions, one attitudinal, the other methodological, for teaching in a postmodern mission context. Modeling learning behavior can help first-term missionaries overcome role deprivations when they think they must put ministry on hold while learning the language and culture. As teachers, pastors and church leaders in many contexts, this kind of attitudinal modeling will also help us modify our current approaches to ministry, teaching and training. If we combine a humble learning posture with greatest storytelling and role-playing, we will be more successful to train leaders and make disciples in today's postmodern context.

Missions, which is the fulfillment of the Great Commission of (Matthew 28:18-20), is part and parcel of the Christian faith. A theological, exegetical, and practice approach has been adopted to study the subject, with due cognizance given to the history of missions and the observations and proposals of experience missionaries. This biblical holistic understanding of missions will have profound effect upon the local church ministry and approach of missions. The local church is not only to be a mission minded but to be involved in missions by engaging in a definite program of local outreach and wider church planting. An awareness of global mission ranging from the tribal urban outreach, Homogeneous to cross cultural evangelism, and past to present practice will give one a sense of direction, purpose and destiny. There is no better way to glorify God then to build up the church of Jesus Christ, by serving in a good local church that is involved in missions. Intended as a textbook on missiology, it is expected that this book will be helpful also to pastors, missionaries, and serious Christians of all denominations.

It will be many new challenges, in the postmodern age of faith. And one of those challenges will be global missions. It will be impossible to move into the postmodern age about understanding and importance of role missions that will play a major part in the preaching of the gospel abroad. It will be impossible to carry out the plan of Christ without understanding the importance of global mission in its entirety to the gospel, and the spreading of the gospel locally, nationally and internationally. Global mission is some of the most difficult work on the planet. Yet, a very needed an integral part, of spreading the gospel in the postmodern age of missions.

Have you ever just paused and considered immersed challenge of global missions? meaning, have you really tried to wrap your head around and understand the overarching purpose and end goal of global missions? When you do consider all that goes into this monumental task, you realize that, in many ways, global missions are some of the most difficult work on the planet. Global mission requires an inescapable element of sacrifice for the sender and for those sent. In the book of acts, the church in Antioch, under the Spirit's guidance, sent the first missionaries (Acts 13:1-4). One can only imagine the sense of sacrifice but by the elders in Antioch as they fasted, pray, and lay hands on Saul and Barnabas before sending them all on that inaugural missionary journey. Moreover, the reality is the same, perhaps even more acute, for those who are sent out today as missionaries. Leaving behind family, friends' vocational identity, familiar environment, and, in some cases, modern, conveniences to cross geographic, cultural, and/or linguistic barriers can be extremely challenging. Thus, the sense of sacrifice for both the sender and the sent want is noteworthy and extraordinary.

Perhaps the most difficult challenges of all global mission are the inevitable worldview clash that takes place every time missionaries try to share the gospel of Christ.

FAITH WORLDVIEW CLASH

The apostle Paul reminded the Christians in Ephesus that the fight is not against flesh and blood, but against the rules, against the authorities, against the cosmic powers of this darkness, against evil, spiritual forces in the heavens. Every time the gospel of Christ is presented in an Asian marketplace, or an African desert, or a European café there's a class a worldview taking place. The missionary, the one sent out from a local church as an ambassador of Christ presents the timeless truths that inevitably collides with the myths, lies, and the predominant worldview of those in the host culture.

The worldview clash manifests itself in a variety of ways. Sometimes, hearer' hearts and ears are closed to the truth. Other times, people will become agitated and angry about the truth shared by the missionary. But sometimes, people's hearts are softened, and the Holy Spirit is moving and works in a unique way as the gospel narrative unfolds. In all of it, one must remember there's a real spiritual battle taking place every time the gospel is proclaimed. In the end, the goal of the worldview clash is a fundamental change in thinking and living.

To acknowledge belief in the gospel in many parts of the world signifies a rejection of what had been believed and practiced in some context for thousands of years. Embracing the gospel is often received by the surrounding community as an acceptance of a foreign religion often with historical baggage and a line of thinking that doesn't mesh or makes sense with their particular worldview. The worldview clash is presenting a variety of significant challenges and obstacles to mission work.

Suffice to say, global mission is to have some of the most difficult work on the planet. They are myriad challenges and hardships related to carrying out the missionary task, but those hardships can be met with an enduring hope.

In the face of all the difficulty and harsh as mentioned above, missionaries are reminded that the only hope they had is found in Christ and in his providential and sovereign work in the world. Missionary tasks, for all the reasons mentioned above, it is impossible from a human perspective.

The good news is that God doesn't operate and work with the human limitations. He's all-powerful, all-knowing, and everywhere present. He has the power and ability to change hearts, change minds, and transform lives. That recognition and reality changes everything and gives missionaries the sending churches an enduring hope that enables them to persist and persevere as they give their time, energy, and lives to the most difficult work on the planet. Global missions.

Never in mission history has the world existed as it does today, never have the opportunities for harvest been so favorable, and never has the need for mobilization been so urgent!

Through the amazing efforts of the missionaries laboring in the first and second eras of the Martin missionary movement (1792-1980), the Church and the non-West has grown1% Evangelical population, to around 70% today.

For the church in those first two eras the challenges were great, but the task was very clear, there were missionary sending countries and missionary receiving countries. Missions from the west to the Rest. E3 (distant peoples) missions was the only option and missions was the task of the full-time missionary professionals.

Fast-forward to our generation and we find the world today very different place. There is a harvest to be brought in, it's the task remaining of some 7000 unreached people groups (UPGs), which presents the most gospel resistant of all the people on the planet. However, today, thanks to the efforts of those pioneer the missionaries the church now exists on every continent that and in every country of the world. And thanks to the globalization the church and the unreached now exist side-by-side, in close proximity to each other (close geographical and often culturally).

For the first time in mission history, reaching unchurched people and seeking breakthrough harvest, can best be achieved through E2 (near- neighbor) missions as opposed to E3 (distant peoples).

Now near neighbor missions could result in breakthrough harvest! Near neighbor missions should be prioritized as a strategy in our day! Traditional (E3) missions will continue, and indeed, need to. There will be some situations where E3 is the only option possible, however, this will increasingly be the exception. The rule will be near neighbor (E2) missions!

For this near neighbor protected to be fully realized, mobilization is the single most critical component. It is needed to help all believers catch and internalized the truly biblical worldview that God has reconciled us to himself and has given us the ministry of reconciliation, God is making his appeal through us (2 Corinthians 5:18-20). It is needed to help change the perception that missions are always a result of air travel to a distant country and for churches to realize that cross-cultural training needs to be a standard part of every churches discipleship program. It is no coincidence that God is emphasizing the emergence and formation of this lost tribe of the church, at the same time as global conditions favor the entirely different approach for world missions.

The culturally relevant ministries in the postmodern world. Will be vastly important and cannot be overlooked to the success of faith in the postmodern age. The importance of relevant ministries cannot be taken for granted especially as new churches are being planted throughout the global world. To be relevant in the postmodern age, will be important and cannot be overlooked, but must be and will be the key, too faith in the postmodern age. So, the question is how relevant must ministries be?

A fascinating movement has been born. Postmodern churches have begun to spring up across North America. They had been described in different terms, postmodern, Gen-X even the overused contemporary. Leonard Sweet refers to those as Noah's Dove Churches because they are testing the waters to how to reach a postmodern North America.

They are predominantly though not exclusively young, and their services are gear towards person looking for different experiences. Spotty reports of these churches can be found on the Internet and in some limited magazines. But no large-scale study has been undertaken.

This is tricky; in a culture that thrives on diversity and disdains uniformity, there is no right way to plant a postmodern church. There is no single answer to reaching postmodernist because there is no one, stereotypical, North America postmodern.

Postmodernism do not fit into a nice little culture box, but most people with a postmodern mindset had this in common: they need to be reach with the gospel of Jesus Christ, and the current pattern of church isn't teaching them.

Despite the obvious difficulty of defining postmodernist, there are some similar patterns in their thinking and feelings. They are almost universal values held by most postmodernist (note the double caveat). Helping to plant an indigenous church is a lot more than a science, but missionaries around the world do it every day. One thing is very clear: postmodernist is different from the people churches have reached successfully in the past. If we write them all as beyond help, as some churches seeing inclined to do, we will ignore the great commission.

New congregation effectively reaching postmodernist. These may be new worship services within an entirely churches, intended to meet postmodernist 'needs, or entirely new congregations. Styles of expression changed between eras; new churches should reflect the change of styles without any change of substance. Patterns are emerging that fit this changing yet unchanging paradigm.

There is a definite need for churches and church services geared towards postmodern. Few boomers or older adults would want to sit in a church service geared towards postmodern. Why would we expect that postmoderns would wish to sit in the service geared towards older adults? Postmodern generations are turning away from institutional Christianity in a way not seen in several generations. This is not because of the gospel as many postmodern responds eagerly to Jesus, but it is because of the traditional culture of the institutional church itself. Church planters who are committed to communicating Christ, who are immersed in the postmodern culture, and who do not feel constrained by traditional patterns of the old church will be the best change agents.

Postmoderns do congregate in certain social centers, but they are different from community to community. According to the survey, the most common places where postmodern church planter build relationship is where most would expect, at the coffee shop. For that reason, planters could assume that the coffee shop in the culture district of any given town is a good place to find postmodern, but that might not be true and every case. Postmodernism is the reigning cultural paradigm in popular media. Postmodern values touch all those who are exposed to popular the media, that is, everyone who watches television! This is virtually everyone.

Faith in the postmodern world will not be void of the spirituality that exist in the spreading of the gospel of Jesus Christ. Postmodern age will be an age that will embrace the Spirit of God unlike the modern age. It would not be an age of carnal and weary faith, but a strong faith in the word of God. This will be key value in the traits of successful postmodern churches, a new progressive generation filled with the Spirit. Being unashamedly Spiritual!

Churches that are reaching postmoderns have not that postmoderns are open to the spiritual. Douglas Coupland, who coined the term Generation X, wrote in Live After God, my secret is that I need God that I am sick and can no longer make it alone.

People have grown tired of the modern believe that everything can be answered by science and reason. They are open to something mystical and spiritual. A hunger for the spiritual runs rampant in postmodern pop culture from Hollywood to politics, spirituality is at a popular high.

Postmoderns are unashamedly proud of their spiritual quests. Postmoderns hold believes in many things, including astrology, new age, tarot cards, psychics, ESP, challenging spirits, reincarnation, witchcraft, palm reading, UFO and aliens, mother earth, crystal power, and Eastern or African spirituality.

Postmodern pop culture is unashamedly proud to throw spirituality at us. On your next trip to the video store, note the array of spirituality on the shelves. Movies such as Sign, The Matrix, and the City of Angels are a few of the box office hits that illustrate this point. Music has been greatly influenced by postmodern pop culture. Postmodern music has confessed to the world that is also unashamedly spiritual. Georgian chants and other recordings of spiritual music our bestsellers in music stores around the continent if we are to read these understandable spiritual postmodern, we must take note of that concept and believes that do not fit within an evangelist goal worldview. Paul's approach to the Athenians. Remember that Paul did for Thane in his effort to be culturally relevant: He understood the Athenians position on reality. He understood an underlying spiritual interest. He looked for positive points with and their worldview. He encouraged them to find true fulfillment in Christ.

Most postmoderns want a spirituality that is authentic above all else. A true postmodern spirituality does not have to be perfect, but it must be genuinely and humbly held. The authenticity of the faith, and that it is sincerely held, is more important than the rational basis of the faith.

The most surprising news of the postmodernity is that postmoderns all or a spiritual search and not an intelligent quest. They are willing at times to take that quest with Christians, if they are genuine and live a holistic faith. If their worship service and small group embraces a participative spirituality, there participation might lead to a genuine faith experience.

Stiver believes that this news is not all bad for Christianity. He explains that being free from the confines of reason has rated a great opportunity for reason dialogue between faith and the world. One agrees churches that will reach postmodern generations need to give evidence of biblical spirituality, drawing from the rich spiritual resources of the Bible and even church tradition.

Finally, the resurrection of Jesus Christ means that we worship and adore a living Christ. He continues to cleanse us from guilt, to create in us a new life, and to bring us as sons and daughters into the family of God. The resurrection and ascension mean that all powers in heaven and earth are subject to our Lord. The truest goodness is the supreme power.

The Christian faith is faith and one who went through death and life to become the living Lord, the vital and effective Presence in the company of believers. Through the Spirit, the risen Lord is present to his followers in a more intimate way than he was in the days when you walk the roads of Galilee and the streets of Jerusalem. The church has found and continue to find his promise fulfilled: I am with you always, to the close of the age (Matthew 28:20).

Jesus Christ, crucified and risen, is the final authority for the Christian and the church. Christians and the church gladly acknowledge that they belong to him. They acknowledged his gracious sovereignty, which is based both on God's approval and on the completeness of his self-giving our good. He is a living Lord, who exercises a threefold Lordship over the Christian, over the Christian church, and over the whole cosmos.

Jesus Christ is the Christian's living Lord who is the norm and the source of spiritual life. He is the final authority, the standard, of the Christian life. Have this mind among yourselves, which you have in Christ Jesus (Philippians 2:5). He is the one through whom we are given forgiveness of sins, the power of a new life, and hope in God. Through sharing in him, God's purpose for us is realized and we are what we ought to be.

Christ is the living Lord of the Christian church, for he is the source and sustainer of its fellowship. He is the Head of the church's;

he exercises the decisive authority in the church. Indeed, the church is the community which acknowledges his Lordship and proclaims that Lordship to man.

He is the living Lord of heaven and earth. His kingdom is holy the is destined to be triumphant over every other power. God has made him sit at the right hand in the heavenly places, far above all rule and authority and power and dominion, and above every name that is named, not only in this age but also in that which is to come; and he has put all things under his feet and has made him the head over all things (Ephesians 1:20b-22). Some indication of this grand cosmic sweep of these words can be conveyed by putting them this way: The Spirit of Jesus Christ is stronger than the powers of nature and stronger than the powers of history. His Spirit is the spirit of the Ultimate. His Spirit is the final power and meaning of the universe.

Christian faith does not affirm that the rule of Christ over all the forces in the universe is obvious. The Christian community knows very well that Christ kingdom is not visible now. The Christian, instead of saying, I have achieved perfection, says with Paul, not that I have already obtained this becoming like Christ in his death or am already perfect; but I press on to make it my own (Philippians 3:12). The Christian church knows only too painfully well it spots and blemishes, it imperfections and ambiguities, and even is failures and loyalty to his Lord. But it looks forward to its certification, to becoming holy and without blemish. Its hope, which is say, its assured confidence, is that in God's own time, the victory of Christ over all the enemies of God will be manifested.

The present hidden Lordship of Christ will become visible, and the kingdom of Christ, already a reality, what have is open triumph over all opposition. The living Lord is the Lord who is to come in victorious consummation of his kingdom. Belief in the final coming of our Lord is the conviction that all things will be brought to acknowledge his sovereignty and therefore the expression of the conviction that we at all men are responsible to him. Thus, we confess in the words of the Apostle Creed: who will come to judge the living and the day.

CONCLUSION

Time and eternity still belong to God. And the postmodern age of faith has not changed this inevitable fact of truth that time and eternity will still belongs to God. This postmodern age of faith will bring to light that the just shall live by faith. God is all-knowing and a very present God despite the time that presents itself. Yesterday today and forever more. So as the kingdom of God prepared itself to operate in faith and by faith receive the blessings of God.

Something more is coming! Everything in Scripture points to it and everything within us cries out for it. God's work with us is not finished in this life. We have already seen authentic Christianity is far more than a pie in the sky, and by and by religion. It is magnificently designed for life on earth, right now, with all its pressures and problems, is joys and tears. But there is yet more. The Apostle Paul sees it as additional ground for confidence and courage. He states plainly that what we are going to do now is getting ready for something yet to come, something so glorious and so different from what we had known that it is beyond our comparison. In the words of Robert Browning and Rabbi Ben Ezra centuries later, and yet in a way more to them Browning ever intended, Paul is saying: grow old along with me! The best is yet to be, the last of life, for which the first was made.

This is the Christian hope. Is more than merely looking onto life beyond the grave. It declares that everything was happens to us in this life is directly related to what is coming, in fact, it is getting us ready for it. Nothing, then, is purposeless or futile in our present experience. It is all necessary to the ultimate end.

This will be an exciting time, for the kingdom of God, and to all those who enter by faith. The postmodern era of faith will be a revolution, that seeks to evangelize the world for Christ. This will be like no other time in the history of mankind. As we turn towards the final stages of the earth the realm it will be in faith, and by faith that we experiences the postmodern age of genuine faith to a generation of believers for the first time in the history of the church which still represents the kingdom of God on earth. Faith in the postmodern age is here! So, let us embrace it for the glory of God.

We will truly become missionaries to a postmodern age of extraordinary faith. One way to regain our passion may be to view the commands of Jesus the way the early church did. The commissioning of Jesus. The Great Commission in Matthew 28, the first and most obvious principle, is Christ first instruction was states that the church is the body under orders by Christ to share the gospel with the whole world.

This will be the age of great evangelism, and faith, that will spread throughout, as you see new churches rising spiritually and physically, they are coming for the lost. The Savior has not given up on His church. An old promise. We are only at the very beginning of a groundswell that is about to sweep across America in the early twenty century. A new look. The church of the twenty century will not look like the typical church of the twentieth century. A different culture calls for a different way in which we see Christ through faith, this is the methodology Christ came to set in place, not just then, not just now, but forevermore.

The great commission presents concentric circles through with to share the gospel (Acts 1:8): Jerusalem, Judea, Samaria, and the world. The center should be called the church's Jerusalem, the equivalent of a hometown or immediate surrounding the congregation. The first circle from center is Judea, which might be identified as one's association, country, or state. The Samaria circle perhaps describe a distinct at the or language group then lies a geographical distance or cultural distance from Jerusalem. The third of final concentric circle represents the world, every place where the name of Christ remains unclaimed. All of these four echelons for evangelism also identify forums in which a church might operate in complete faith in the marketplace.

Perhaps as we combined the power of the Spirit and Spirit led systems, church planting movements can emerge in North America. My prayer, now that you have read this, it is God will to bless you as you begin this journey of planting his church. May God guide and empower you. In the words of Christian history's great church planter, Now to him who is able to do immeasurably more that all we can ask or imagine, according to his power that is at work within us, to him be glory in the church and in Christ Jesus throughout all generations, forever and ever! Amen (Ephesians 3:20-21)

May God lead you to plant churches. There can be no greater task then evangelizing and congregationalism North America. As we join God in this task, we become missional on mission with God to see his kingdom expanded. We become participants in the missio dei. Who knows what God will do through us! In the postmodern age of the faith we proclaim.

Yes, if you believe in the resurrection that is continuous, one that will ultimately bring about the resurrection of your total life, through the proclamation of faith, you will believe in miracles for the now.

Now is faith that's what the Bible says. And the resurrection of Jesus Christ was not an accident. The resurrection opened the door for faith to operate always, operate in the now. Now is faith! For the postmodern age.

The faith we are proclaiming today, is the resurrection power of Jesus Christ! And it is contagious, for the postmodern age of faith!

Dr. M. Nathaniel Anderson. Ph.D.

BIBLIOGRAPHY

Elmer J.F. Arndt, Book, The Faith We Proclaim (The Christian Education Press, 1961) 8-10

Dr. Harold A Carter, The Mission of the Church (Mission, New Shiloh Church, 1993) 14-15

Elmer J.F. Arndt, Book, The Faith We Proclaim (The Christian Education Press, 1961) 11-13

Gregory W. Hall, Living the Faith, The Nicene Creed for a Postmodern Age, (Parson's Porch & Company, 2020) 1-2

Dennis Culbreth, Voices of Faith; Living A Christian Life in a Postmodern World (Chattanooga Times Free Press, 2016) 3

Kurt Struckmeyer, A Life of Faith in a Postmodern World (Wipf & Stock Publisher Eugene, Oregon, 2016) 1-4

Carlo Maria Martini, Teaching the Faith in a Postmodern World, (America Magazine, 2008) 1-6

Hamzah Zahid, Talking About Faith in the 21st Century, (Interfaith Now/Medium, 2019) 1-5

Submitted by anonymous, Postmodernism: The Spirit of the Age, (Xenos Christian Fellowship, 2020) 1-4

Kurt Struckmeyer, The Postmodern World. (Wipf & Stock Publishers Eugene Oregon, 2017) 1, 5, 8

Gregory W Hall, Living the Faith: The Nicene Creed for a Postmodern Age (Parson's Porch & Company, 2020) 1-2

Karl Barth, Book by David L Mueller, Maker of the Modern Theological Mind (Word Book Publisher, Waco Texas, 1972) 37-40

General Observations and Recommendations, Living Our Faith in the 21st Century, (Justice & Charity & Stewardship, 2008) 3

Aubrey Malphurs, Book, Planting Growing Churches for the 21st Century, (Baker Book House, 1992) 157

Thom Rainer, Book, Effective Evangelistic Churches, (Broadman & Holman Publishers, 1996) 168

Robert E. Coleman, Book, The master plan of Evangelism (Revell Baker Book House, 1963) 36-37

Paul Mumo Kisav, What Postmodernism Means for Evangelism, (Lausanne World Press Pulse Archives, 2007) 3-5

Thom Rainer, Book, Effective Evangelistic Churches, (Broadman & Holman Publishers, 1996) 168

Michael McCoy, Community: A Postmodern Mission Paradigm (Published online by Cambridge Community Press, 2009) 1

Ronald T. Michener, Missionary Teaching in a Postmodern Context (Mission Nexus, 2005) 1-2, 13

Boom-Sing Poh, Anthological, Exegetical and Practical Perspective of Mission (Publisher Good News Enterprise, 2019)

Max Chrismon, Understanding the Nature of Mission Today (Second Mile N2, 2020) 1-2

Ed Stetzer, Book, Planting New Churches in Postmodern Age (Breadman & Holman Publishers, 2003) 130-133

Paul Akin, 5 Considerable Challenges for Today's Missionary (Church Planting, 2019) 1-3

Elmer J. F. Arndt, Book, The Faith We Proclaim (The Christian Education Press, 1961) 56-58

Ray C. Stedman, Book, Authentic Christianity (Word Book, Wasco Texas, 1975) 126-127

Ed Stetzer, Planting New Churches in Postmodern Age (Broadman & Holman Publishers, 2003) 321, 336

Printed in the United States
by Baker & Taylor Publisher Services